Sweet Air

January 2013

Dorothy,

may you have a blessed
new year ahead of you.

with love,

Charlotte

Sweet Air

poems

Charlotte Mears

There are the days when Birds come back—
A very few—a Bird or two—
To take a backward look.

—Emily Dickinson

Sweet Air Press

Madison, Mississippi

Design by Lucy Stovall and Charlotte Mears
Cover art by Jim Lawler, 2012
Printed by Hederman Brothers, Ridgeland, Mississippi

ISBN 978-0-9855904-0-6

for my daughter, Emily Grace

Making Way

It starts as if arranging a space for a welcome guest,
the thoughtful, beautiful young woman you have become.
I stand in your room, looking for the things you've outgrown.

Contents

One

Woman in the Bathhouse   3

Sundays   4

Breath Held and Holding Still   5

False Spring   6

Out Looking to Move, Manhattan   7

What the Mind Holds, a Constant Surprise   8

In the Middle of Routine, a Source Comes   9

Coming Home   10

Ablution   11

Orr's Island, Maine, August 1959   12

Swoon, Atlanta, Georgia   17

Tornado Watch, Tuscaloosa, Alabama   18

Furrawn   19

Boy Up to His Neck, Coney Island   20

Adolescence Recalled   22

Imprints   23

Eluded   24

Two

Nuance   27

Out of My Hands, Austin, Texas   28

Long Distance   30

This Is Not the Life I Had Imagined   31

Drowse, Hollins, Virginia   32

Speech of the Heart   33

Hill Country in April, Mason, Texas   35

Things That Recall Us   36

Looking for Dinosaur Bones   37

Almost Spring, Starkville, Mississippi   39

Again   41

Hung Over in Good Weather,
    Silver Lake Park, Staten Island   42

Never Again   43

Ladder to the Moon   44

In the Presence of Small Occurrences   46

Intruder   47

Are We Awake or Only Dreaming   48

Three

Call and Response 53

Just a Couple of Wings, Fayetteville, Arkansas ... 54

Morning Calls 56

First Frost 58

Torn 59

Discernment 60

Practice in Gratitude 61

Like This 62

Things Seen and Unseen 63

Nobody Dies 64

All Souls, East Aurora, New York 67

Contraction, Release 68

Revisions 69

Jackson Square, New Orleans,
   New Year's Eve Following Hurricane Katrina .. 71

Under the Weather, Yaddo, Saratoga Springs, New York .. 72

Whole Hog 74

On This Day 76

Once More, Before Dismantling the Dollhouse .. 77

Notes 81

Acknowledgments 83

. . . late one night,
I saw the icon of a man
trying to breathe like me, his mouth
puckered for the sweet air—
to take it into his body . . . .

—John Clellon Holmes, "Samoan Head"

One

Woman in the Bathhouse

after Andrew Wyeth's painting *Off at Sea*

Four sweatered figures appear on the beach below.
One, a small boy, stands in front
of a girl with his arms raised,
a gesture for her to pull his sweater off.
As she pulls the wool neck over his face
he falters as if his own skin were rising
over his head like a black hood.
The bathhouse has five sets of windows
overlooking the bay. The afternoon sun
falls in rectangles on the deacon's bench
that lines the wall beneath them.
All is white and gray, even the heavy
clouds seem to look in. My shadow stretches
across the yellow pine floor while I sit
sideways on the bench, looking out.
Mine is the only sweater hung on a hanger
from a row of hooks on the wall.
Two of the figures bend over something
on the beach while the boy dances
hyphenated circles around them, tapping
their backs with a stick. Down at the water's
edge, the girl points toward the bathhouse.
The figures straighten and the boy falls
to the sand. Turning to the girl, then toward
the bathhouse, a woman lifts a hand to her forehead
while the other, a man, cups both hands around
his mouth as if to call. Even the boy points.
They all begin to wave in long sweeping movements.
I pull my sweater, making the hanger swing through
its own shadow. I can't look at their faces hard enough.

Sundays

An unlit chapel after services,
after the sexton's last round,
the oak doors bolted shut,
there is this smell of pink face powder,
hair tonic, and ironed clothes,
and there is this silence
that shifts from one hip to the other—
an ache that can almost be described,
almost located like a splinter
of glass beneath the skin.
And there is this solitary candle
that is never allowed to go out,
must never go out.

Breath Held and Holding Still

As if breathing would break
the trace tenderness leaves—
a spider's web stretched how far?
Only parts of its thread caught
and tossed up by light and breeze.

So much has fallen—
your eyes around mine, your mouth.
The sound of your approach
across the back field now
a dry leaf turned by wind.

How quickly the mind slips
from flesh on flesh—
it crosses my mind, not in the shapes
suggested, but in the shape
of the crow flapping.

In the space you have created
a bathtub recalls the slow lap
of your bathing and the smell
of your skin, damp clay,
saddening round.

Piece by pleasing piece of you
merges with wintry air—
the mind stretches for the length of you.
Held and holding, the faucet's drip,
the sudden wasp, his banging need.

False Spring

The hardwoods are not so easily roused.
Oh, but the Japanese magnolia blooms
six thick fleshy petals
tinted pink and lavender
each blossom borne singly
at twig's end against an indifferent blue
as if to defy a foreseeable future—
carpe diem!—as if to display an arousal
love makes as they open
toward the promise of longer light—
so vulnerable, inevitably spent in their profusion.

Out Looking to Move, Manhattan

My decision turns with ill-fitting keys
locks of doors that open into
the not-yet neutral scent of vacancy,
opens the peculiar sense of intrusion
as the odor of another life not yet lifted stirs.

One armchair sits plump by a window.
Under the seat cushion, no coin, paper clip,
pencil, not even a hair, only the presence of the one
I most imagine—alone, contented, reading by alley light.
One wild guess at the reason for her moving,

and there are the two of us standing mutely,
looking less for a suitable space and more for what we
mean but don't say—a continuity that dropped out
quietly along the way, one that reverberates
within our restless, discrete lives.

What the Mind Holds, a Constant Surprise

Not with hands exactly, or a bowl,
more as a window holds a landscape
shimmering with a slope beyond view—
there are blue barns so sudden
they stick. Blue barns reflecting
a blue so blue, fields rise up to them,
pulling blue trees with them.
Like the circle of water rising
around a dropped stone
collapses and sends a stamen of water up
to fall through itself, blue barns fall
and rise and rise again
beyond a window that welcomes
blue barns in.

In the Middle of Routine, a Source Comes

At the sink
washing a bowl

its smooth shape
traced and swabbed by my fingers

feeling for rough spots
under running water

suddenly here is Kerry
many moons earlier

at her crowded sink
me sitting at a glass table

talking together in early spring light
she cradles a blue bowl in one hand

her thumb follows the inside curve
fingers slide deep into the center

like our running conversation
running clear as water

we shake a bowl once
set it down to dry

joined by our mindful business at hand.

for Kerry Wooten

Coming Home

I hear Mother
carry her fear through
the rooms of this stone house.
There, in the darkest corner
of the den, she sat
upright, unable to lie down,
the cancer too tight across
her flattened chest.

Ah, but when she moved, she moved at first
to the memory of waltzes and dresses cut low,
but coming stiff again
against her dying,
she angled forward
up the stairs

closed the door
of a spare room,
to undress without looking.
She cleaned herself
with towels and ointments,
came out thicker-chested,
spooled in gauze,
under the shirts,
under her wrinkled dress.

I look into this house.
I see my mother's face
instead of my shadow there
in the front door glass
asking, *What took you so long?*

Ablution

At least I have the flowers of myself,
and my thoughts, no god
can take that.
                    —H.D.

From the center of bed
I reach across
the even sheets
and lift the curtain
away from the sill
The sky is smooth
as a porcelain basin
I listen to the evenness
of my breath as I slide
an egg from a spoon
into boiling water
and watch as the egg
spreads and hardens
Its singularity
pleases me
I sponge bathe
over the sink
while looking at Degas'
Woman at Her Toilette
and watch as we wash
until we come back
to ourselves
wash down to the center
of ourselves
to wash singularly
and wash down
to a common skin

Orr's Island, Maine, August 1959

I

Between turns in sleep,
I measured the trip to Maine
by the telephone wire
that increased and decreased
in thickness
outside the car window.
I entertained myself,
imagined two cartoon characters
who ran on the wire.
A boy chased the homely
girl, her name was Olive,
but just as he reached for the tip
of her skirt, she seemed to fly off
like a rose-breasted grosbeak
and settled on top of a widow's walk
in the town square of Harpswell.

We stopped in Mr. Moody's General Store
and he showed us his tank
of green lobsters.
I pressed my hands against the glass
and looked in
through bits of floating algae.
I wanted to remove the wooden pin
from each lobster's claw.
But Father pointed,
and Mr. Moody scooped
them out with a net
into a brown paper bag.

Past Mrs. Hotchkin's, past
the meetinghouse, we took
the dirt road paved
with a year's growth
of weeds and wild grass.
First the chimney of our cottage
rose through the pines.
Then we came to a clearing—
alongside the porch,
a wooden raft propped up
against the pump.

Mother went to unlock the door,
Father got his saw from the shed,
my brothers inspected their hand-built raft.
I ran down the overgrown
path to Lowell's Cove,
to a rock much larger than I.
Climbing onto it,
I felt the blue veins in the white quartz,
looked closely
to see if the pinks were still there.

II

But that summer there was something else.

It was a seal,
swept into the cove
by late summer tides,
rotting out of shape.
I wondered what it had had in its belly
the moment before the daze,
the confusion swept it under and away.
Where are its eyes and mouth now?

Father and I dug a grave,
and I thought
I saw the Dead Ship of Harpswell
drift out to sea, stern first
against wind and tide.

III

My brothers made toy boats from balsa
and sails from rags stored
under the summer sink.
They sailed them from the pier we built
while I pulled open mussels,
stubborn mussels,
for the imperfect pearl.

Father taught me how to recognize
the pinhole bubbles of clams in sand.
I dug, dug, dug,
but my mind was still on the seal
ten yards away.
I tried to measure its decay
with stick and pole
and began to see its hidden, inner symmetry.

Mother and I went raspberry and blackberry
picking every midmorning,
plucking the juicy, firm heads
into our buckets and mouths.
Then we went for cream
from the dairy down the road—
I remember the cows standing in straw,
their tails made rows of fly swatters and manure,
and below, the milk and cream we came for.

IV

Bowls, white bowls, blue bowls
filled with berries,
swimming in cream.
Our silver spoons dug, dug, dug.
Then clams and lobsters, steaming
in more bowls, covered with pearls.
Grosbeaks with pearls between
their beaks, delivering one for each widow,
each grave already dug for a corpse
that has not yet arrived,
that won't settle in new ground.

The seal had been washed up again,
rotting out of shape.
Another grave dug,
this time only its torso
covered with sand and driftwood.

Mother, are you there with the seal now?
Have you finished shifting and settling?

V

One morning I saw Mother
from my bedroom window
drawing water from the pump.
She filled two glass jugs,
wrung out our beach towels,
and took a drink from her cupped hands.

What was it that always got you up
before the rest of us?

I saw you take off your watch
and relax beneath the birch tree.
You looked so young—
your skirt above your knees
while you rested your back against the tree.
But you got up too soon.
What was it, Mother?
Some inner wing, beating awake?
Perhaps you felt silly
in such abandon.
But I knew you that morning—
a dreamy girl with pink knees.

You were a bowed stem,
springing from the wet grass
as you arched your back and walked to the cottage.

Seals, mussels, cream, berries—
we pass and return to that place
where there is a breaking
a second before change.

In memoriam, Grace Kathleen Mears, 1916–1973

Swoon, Atlanta, Georgia

I look to the tops of trees,
the straight pines risen like sticks
in the narrow spaces of light,
how they have fitted themselves
and thrived limber, sway
their whole thin length
by gusts of wind and breezes alike.
A downy woodpecker clings and lines
his spotted breast to shingled bark,
his nature to carve out two nest cavities
and yield to his mate to choose.
He cocks his head in my direction,
sensing my gaze behind the window?
then resumes his rapid drilling, uncovering
busy pockets of insects unaware,
their linear work interrupted, a scattering,
their panic for cover lost on the deference he shapes.
Laid bare, we, each to each.

Tornado Watch, Tuscaloosa, Alabama

Thunder shakes the whole house.
I hold onto our rented
bed, my only life raft,
while the man who lives
outside the window at night,
the one you never see,
watches me struggle with sleep.
Certain the watch will
turn into a warning,
I locate candles and matches
thinking when all else fails
this light will keep me safe.
I pull the spring blanket
up to my chin
prepared to block
the lightning's illumination.
But my timing's off.
The window lights up
his obscene baby face
pink against the wet
black umbrella.
He gestures for me
to let him in then laughs.
His continuous laughter
falls like the rain
from the gutterless roof.
The old terror of sleeping alone—
I click off the lamp,
listen for the funnel cloud's approach,
the swift silent unlocking,
his seductive watery breath
next to mine.

Furrawn

Tell me again the meanings
of *sleepy* and *tired*.
I want to feel
the pressures
of your words
and their falling away,
like the holding
then letting go
of hands before sleep.
By the definition
of your hand beside mine,
I ask beyond our forgettable sleep.

Boy Up to His Neck, Coney Island

Families set up their versions
of the good life, defining their spots
on the beach by blanket, towel, or cooler,
and relinquish themselves
to the sun and murky surf.

But not you, a boy not big enough
to be ten, not small enough to be five,
and not me. While watching my friend
bury his child in the sand taking the shape
of her body like a cast, knitting

them together by their unspoken play,
you fall to your knees in front of me,
grab fistfuls of sand like black money
and ask, *What they doing?* Before I can respond,
you pin me down with what tumbles out of your mouth:

From Puerto Rico three years now,
live in Brooklyn. My father's big and strong
and can hurt anybody! He's 28.
Heard somebody killed here last night.
Cut up bad.

The only smart thing to do. I get up on my knees,
push you gently prone, begin heaping sand
onto your hands and legs and arms, push sand against
your back and sides—

What's in there? jutting your chin toward the ocean.
Why does the water leave?
What's in there, in the sand?
What's underneath?
Why you come here?
How old you are?
I have a long name, J-o-s-e-p-h.
Isn't it long?
I go to Puerto Rico soon.
See my grandmother.
Play with me.

Adolescence Recalled

Rain on Sunday afternoon,
the last altar candle snuffed out,
burned wax, a quiet looms.
I take my place on the top stair,
stare out tall windows to the street.
Except for an occasional car, the neighborhood sleeps.
I wait for rest to come to me as well.
What the world pours into me I can't tell.
I could drown in my own skin without notice.

Imprints

My friend looks always to the horizon
as if it, like a bed sheet, will lift with the wind
and reveal the raw source of his comfort—
rich, alluvial soil of Mississippi Delta
where wet acres rise in soybean and cotton.

Now in Atlanta where dogwoods crowd the view
from his upstairs apartment, he mutters,
Where am I and how did I get here?
while the neighbors' dogs bark and bark and bark
because, he says, dogs don't hear themselves barking.

I tell my friend I'm imprinted by people.
Born into a congregation my father ministered,
I hold the quiet space of parishioners in prayer
and the sharp difference of those who fidgeted and coughed,
fidgeted and cleared their throats in the pews.

No, not here for me either, Wally.
Austin sprawls with live oak, mesquite, cedar.
I'd be pleased by dogwood in bloom instead of what grows brittle
and crooked. Either way, I look out for someone
I can talk with, look long for the indelible bloom of a face.

for Wally Wooten

Eluded

After a trip, after rain,
home again

I smell something sweet
but can't detect its source.

I sniff,
nose up in air,

break off a stem of flowers
from a bush. Not there.

I look to the yard
for new shape and color,

but nothing stirs,
only my nose full of sweet welcome.

Two

Nuance

Blue seen how
through another's eyes?

A steady look
a wave goodbye

each with its own
shade of meaning.

Second guessing like belief itself
what I hold I hold loosely.

Blue is my heart beating
hello hello come closer please.

Out of My Hands, Austin, Texas

My daughter framed in the rearview mirror
goes higher and higher on the schoolyard swing.
She pumps her three-year-old legs and sails
out of sight as I drive away to work
thinking of her swinging too high,
the long chain catching and falling
beyond me, the sound of metal and pebbles, her cry.

I approach a woman carrying a child on her shoulders,
another clutched to her waist. I think to stop
and ask if she needs a ride, check the traffic
behind me, see anyway how she'd refuse
my open door. I drive on leaving their precarious
balance with the hope it delivers them safely, where?

Sudden rain, and a man dressed in suit and tie
stands at the bus stop. I want to toss him
the umbrella on my back seat, but traffic pulls
me along too quickly. He places his briefcase
on top of his head as I pass, as he stretches
in the rain for the sight of his bus.

What couples do in their narrow beds
as they turn toward and away from each other,
a dance performed over the years,
an eventual easeful sleep into dreams playing
through their heads, charged
with separate stories, still, lying side by side.

The gift comes out of my hands
placed on either side of my daughter's head
as I bend down to place a kiss on each soft cheek,
kiss her hopefully,
Did you have fun today? Ready to go?

Tonight fireflies will lift like a slow boil.
It begins low to the ground,
sending columns of light lightly
to a darkening blue.
The yard buzzes with life at summer dusk,
out of my hands too, I embrace.

Long Distance

A line of glass carries a version of my voice
along thousands of others in a stream.
Hi, Dad, this is Charlotte.
(I always tell you who I am to reduce confusion.)
My voice relays with yours along a single fiber—
Well, hello there, Bombi, you reply.
I ask you to think back to Spring of 1939. You are 27.
Did you go to the New York World's Fair or were you
in the Philippines beginning your missionary work?

I have carried you back too far this time.
Your voice comes to me by total internal reflection
like time travel and I become someone else as you ask:
What were you doing in 1938. . .have a job in. . .?
If this glass could break! Is he talking to his sister?
Which sister? Who am I to you in this fragile warp?
Everything's dark and it's as if I'm plunging my arm into a hole
to feel for my father and pull him out, bring him home into this light.
I scramble to cover the fear I have lost you, announce
before you can say anything more, *Dad, I wasn't even born yet!*

I don't know how I recovered or you.
The fiber between us normalized, you, Dad, me, daughter,
we speak of our upcoming family reunion,
end our call with a stream of *Love you, addio.*
Once in a while I allow myself to think of you gone,
slipped away, leaving me broken off from your musical voice.
Death's part of life, you would tell me when I was young.
I hold you on the line,
not ready for you to slip into that final light.

In memoriam, The Reverend John Dominic Mears, 1912–2011

This Is Not the Life I Had Imagined

Today is one of those days
I can't tell if I'm screaming
when I order lunch.
The ice in my tea melted;
it's hard to see this as progression.

Other days I witness
the sacrilege of sorrow
stepping into the bluest
spring sky. No way to step
into the sky's bath naked to the knee.
This sorrow blasts cool waters,
allows nothing, not even the sky
its clear invitation.

Trying to reach a middle ground,
I drive to the coast, pass hawks
steady on the power line and a blue barn
that stands against the mind's movement.

I am divided. Watching the mind
fall then catch itself
after the inevitability of sorrow—

take this sound home then,
the ocean's reminder,
but even this is divided,
twitches like hands remembering,
like the mind watching
for the disappearance of things.

Drowse, Hollins, Virginia

After rain
the sky pink and cool
as shell
fresh out of water
asparagus shoot up
along the length of fences
rusting mailboxes
a bathtub in a field
filling with cows.

A leaf falls
blooms on water
in a creek run
through redbud, dogwood, black willow
lilac in the sky blooming
love so hard
forsythia and fog gather
a field and cover it with hands.

for Richard Dillard

Speech of the Heart

It is so delicate
this impulse to name
the slight stirring
behind the focused eye,
the sudden fall cold
may lift it away
into trees shocked and whipped by wind.

Yellow butterflies tied
bows in the soft light.
A bucket hung
from a chain link fence
cast a shadow like a hand.
My wrist lay across
this fence like the broken
neck of a crane.

Some stop loving
as quietly as snow
falls by streetlamps
at night, carrying
a funeral inside them
like a holiday calm.
I too have admired fruits and nuts
in a bowl, seen a life
as simple as this:
deer hang gutted
from trees. Everything frozen,
iced over, perfect.
A woman dries her hands
at the kitchen sink,

another serves tea
from a blue teapot.
Sunlight patterns the floor.
Lace curtains breathe
as cold wind moves in.
Other hands approach a keyboard.
The fingers stretch and reach
for the keys, poise above them
like white bone china.

I will move inside a wave
where things come quickly
and confuse themselves
under hands, a lover's touch
confused with mine.

I crack open walnuts,
their lungs the shape of ours.
We touch where touch
loses shape.
Here it so delicate
it would hurt to name.
So much in us stirs.

Hill Country in April, Mason, Texas

Shadows splash darkly
across the road to Gooch Cemetery
while fields burst with bluebonnet, Indian blanket,
Mexican hat, wine cup, purple poppy mallow.

Eunice, your mother, is laid to rest,
joins your father, Francis, where the ground
closes up at our backs as we turn away
to the shriek of a red-winged blackbird.

White and purple thistle
and beyond the rise of sandstone hills,
we can't help but think of their hands,
both with brilliant, accomplished hands.

Eunice's small painter hands created landscapes
bright with shape and color,
cadmium orange and lemon sky,
the one we all thought her best,

and Francis's long fingers of entrepreneurial
hands—engineer, printer, farmer, entomologist—
near the end of his life focused on the delicate
azure blue butterflies of South America.

We can't help but think they'll miss how our lives
will change and grow or stay a little the same.
And they will always be with us, nudging us on—
no matter how subtly, how they still urge us to do our best.

for David McCulloch

Things That Recall Us

The bending of limbs in wind
The illuminated doorbell
at night with no one at home
The spiralling shifting fall again
into a face, its flesh recalling bone
Just misses
The penny on the street
All that we have lost, all that begins
to recall us

The neighborhood rings
with telephones
Two dogs whimper
like whipped children
Pigeons flutter flutter
like tires going flat
A woman cuts her lawn
into stripes, a green and dark green
blind against the public eye
A man swims against the far shore
as white water sprays up like whale air
after each kick

On a day before rain
there is this roundness
the fall hum of grass
one crepe myrtle against
the softened fall sky
The sky casts a net
we begin to recognize

Looking for Dinosaur Bones

We clamor into the pickup
and take off down dirt roads
of Texas hill country in search
of the bones we're certain haven't yet
been discovered but lie out clearly
for the discerning eye to see.

Like setting out to look for something
misplaced, you see it in your mind's eye,
trusting if you concentrate on the image
hard enough it will lead you to it—
the odd sock, the key, even the lost
look in the telling skin around eyes
once bright. Where have they gone,
these images set like bone in memory?
How will we find them again?

We stop at an outcrop of pink granite
and begin our excited climb,
each of us taking a slightly different
path between yucca and prickly pear.
One finds a vein of white quartz
running like a scar across the rock's surface,
while another points out tiny transparent
fish swimming in standing water
pooled in the indentation there.

Like looking for something you've already found,
what we imagine is ours is ours already.
There's no taking the discovery away,
no loss at all, unless we demand to touch

the porousness of bone—teeth, jaw, skull.
But we know better. Our desire runs like veins

in us and we come down off the rocks with fistfuls
of stones, fragments of bone we reconstruct
to fit the occasion of this Thanksgiving.
The truck throws up dust as we set out into the sunset,
purples, pinks, oranges, a startling blue,
and beyond, satiated by our findings, human, huge,
far from extinction and warming in our hands.

for Alex and Emily McCulloch

Almost Spring, Starkville, Mississippi

Almost spring and a hammer
falls on posts for fences
that go up again
around a neighbor's garden.
High-pitched syllables
of children slip
between playground monkey bars.

A neighbor woman
stands in her yard
holding a pail
her feet stuffed
into red sneakers
her breasts on her belly
under the pink shift.

Stopped still like this
on her slow walk
to the spigot
she plants herself
on the beige lawn
and looks up
sharing the sky in common.

A warm front moves
across the sky like a barge
and a swell of clouds in its wake.
Flags fly at right angles.
The one plane may take us away
to another version of spring.
A voice recalls us.

A blending of iron on wood
singular and true
as the child's voice
that rings above the others
rolls over them
like a marble in play.
Starlings swarm the sky
and the earth spins and spins.

Again

Today I will tell the truth.
It begins in the mouth of a kiss

wanting another and another after
kisses that promised to be the last.

It hesitates between sentences,
unsure of what it has just said,

stands stock still between the tongue,
the roof of the mouth, and the long

mirrored corridor of the throat.
Which way to go?

Swallowed by indecision, it sails
the history of mouths it has entered

and exited like a boat unanchored
floating by tidewater alone,

like the memory of blues
scaling up the face of the throat

and rappelling down its craggy side,
like hands remembering something

years after the last pitch,
and I'm *Out*, feeling the truth

strike against the back of my teeth,
which are always stunned.

Hung Over in Good Weather,
Silver Lake Park, Staten Island

I try to stretch over this hill
like the bare shadow of trees,
the dark part of themselves
they shake out to air on spring grass.

Lacking their good nature, I lie
out reeking of cigarettes and wine,
a damp mattress in better shape
for the dump than fresh air.

My eyes stagger across the lake
to gulls that flap up to flight
so quick I swear they occupy
both blues of water and sky.

But my head is empty as a gymnasium
with one unathletic kid shooting
baskets off the backboard
all day long into night—

when the ball circles the rim twice
like the wobbly moments before sleep,
drops through the tattered net
into sweaty, grateful hands.

Never Again

Waking up
to the dry mouth
of what was said
last night

sad yellow
adrenalin
that follows
a confession or lie

food-flecked
linen of a dinner table
I push my chair under
and leave

a lingering wish to turn back
take your hand
talk things over
to a better end.

Ladder to the Moon

If love is a painted ladder
on a painted sky
and the moon perfectly halved,
how it got there isn't important.
The ladder most improbably suspended
between mountains and moon
has no roots except in you
who can see the climbing.

You change a light bulb,
hang curtains in windows,
slide into cool blue water
or onto the playground's dust,
step into a cab or combine,
connect drainpipes to gutters,
make a swan dive into an Olympic-sized pool
and come out smiling into the camera.
Get a cat off the roof, paint a barn,
drench a fire, drop into a lifeboat
from the side of a ship, ascend
from a submarine to catch the silver on the night water,
climb a railroad trestle, a silo, a fire tower,
into root cellars, attics, haylofts,
or you're a trapeze artist quickly climbing, sequined.

There are other ladders to climb—
railroad ties in winter, Venetian blinds,
roller coasters, Ferris wheels,
escalators, fishing piers,
ice cube trays, piano keys,

Jacob's Ladder, lunar landers,
ferns, fish fossils, your lover's
fingers, teeth, legs, ribs, spine.

Between each rung, a new sky
you may fall through
but don't. You step easily up
sure of the distances you see.
Nearer the moon, the earth's oceans
brighten blue and green.
This is where you are at last—
stepping off a golden ladder to the moon
you don't fear falling from.

for Ann Oakes

In the Presence of Small Occurrences

Perfectly shaped pyramids of cedar shavings
stand the length of the porch
while in the eaves overhead
female carpenter bees bore inside
their newly rounded holes,
drill tunnels to lay their eggs
as males hover nearby,
ready to buzz a perceived intruder's head,
such as mine.
It is April,
the stinging time.
I count the holes and each correlating
pyramid to the far end of the porch
where days stretch ahead in concert with the single-minded *tick-tick* drilling of bees
It should be so simple.

Intruder

Tonight the dogs jump up and bark
from their respective beds—

one from his mound of leaves,
the other from a living room chair.

What is it this time? Deer, possum, raccoon, or
simply the stray cat who lounges beside the sliding glass door?

Whatever it is, it has crossed a boundary
and the dogs' barking can go on for hours, first one then the other,

as if barking in turn makes a larger, fiercer sound
to keep the intruder at bay, far off in the darkness.

But not tonight. Without looking at the clock,
I feel my way through the hallway door to let out

the inside dog, switch on the outdoor light as both chase
and run together through the curtain of dark.

Floodlights on the grass, the trees, make the yard
look eerily hyperreal, like a stage set, a space

where another character waits in the wings to make its entrance.
I understand their need to bark and run and seek, for the intruder

eggs them on to go farther than what the light allows.
It interrupts our sleep, runs up to the edge

of dream, pleads to be let in.
Maybe this time to grant our tiniest wishes.

Are We Awake or Only Dreaming

We're only particles of change, I know, I know,
orbiting around the sun.

—Joni Mitchell

Heat waves shimmy like spirits off the blacktop
while water bands the road
cool, deep perhaps, each pool
a slick invitation to drive right through
sending up splays of water
then the swish of wet tires on asphalt.

But like the trick of memory beginning
to emerge, we say it's on the tip
of our tongues, and *poof*, it's gone,
memory, like the water, out of reach.

I tell Emily
how the sun's reflection
gathers in pools of sky
on such trips, how the water we see
ahead shimmers like a waking dream.

I tell her, *listen.*
Sometimes at night, a very still night,
windless, you can, if you're lucky, catch
the mirrored trees and moon on water,
hold your breath, and still not know
which is the sky, which its pure reflection.

We travel on high above the blacktop
sharpened for the illusion to show itself,
unwilling to say why
or how
or when
but that it will,
yes, just like that, again.

Three

Call and Response

I

Where do you go when you turn inward?
What meets you there?
Are there hands to welcome you?
Is there touch, a child's touch,
plump and prone across your knuckles?
Could it be your own hand leading you
from room to unkempt room?

Or are there another's hands
touching the small tight
spaces between your fingers
to help open resolve?
Where do you go, in what room do you pause?

II

Here a cluster of images has been laid out—
eyestalk of a blue snail
a hood of skin
the curl of a frightened dog
tired heads bowed over a book or in prayer

handle of a cup, a fist
the jack-in-the-pulpit's arched spathe
the sleep of flamingos, a mock kiss.
See how they can be arranged,
a kind of company they keep.

Just a Couple of Wings, Fayetteville, Arkansas

I like to shoot
so I like these blackbirds,
said the boy who lives
beside these railroad tracks
we walk on in the snow.
He shot one right through
the breast and said as he
pumped his pellet gun again:
I kept one of these birds
in a shoebox with a robin once,
they was both awful sick,
they didn't get along
so the blackbird died real quick.

Then he said to us,
his eyes tracing the trees—
I didn't do nothing wrong.
The blackbird pecked at
the robin's chest
so I wanted to see what
the blackbird would look
like with a red breast.

The boy was called home.
He kicked snow over the bird
he'd just shot, aimed into
the trees once more,
turned and laughed at us—
Just a couple of wings!

More blackbirds fly over
toward the grain elevator.
If only the boy were here now—
look how the trees
are shaped in black,
how they beat and murmur
like hundreds of black hearts.

And over here. There's a broken
wing in the bush. Watch its mad
flutter from branch to ground
to branch again.
Tell us how to pick it up
and how to hold it,
or kill it with a rock.

for David Sanders

Morning Calls

I

The birds alight long enough to consider—
the blue jay's crisp plumage set
against the early spring's branch.
How can anything so blue
function in this world?
Its color's lost on the cat.
For whom does the blue jay come so blue?

A sudden startle intervenes, a cardinal,
his allure a splash of passion,
self-assured, a crowned arrogance.
Above me a yellow spot twitches.
I lean back to see around the branch
and the glare the light makes—
a yellow warbler, his rounded breast streaked
chestnut, just right. Somewhere amidst the grays
and browns of the hardwood's high branches
a mourning dove issues his four notes, *Oo-wah-hooo, hoo-hoo*,
the prelude to his courtship flight.
I respond to another call, Emily's
punctual need of me, go inside where she lies
between dream and wakefulness. *I'm coming, my girl.*

II

For you, I can only imagine.
You pull on your laundered shirt,
the starched slide sounds
across your back and arms
and you begin working the buttons

through each stiffened and narrow hole—
like climbing a small ladder, its rungs
shallower than the length of your foot—
you have to go slow and think of what needs to be done
when you reach the top—add a paragraph,
cancel a lunch date, buy food coloring for the Easter eggs—
but remember there's something
missing you can't put your finger on as you slide
a necktie into place, fold down the back of your collar
and finish with a half-Windsor knot.

What was it? Like the trick of peripheral vision,
something flickered in and out of sight,
a suggestion of wholeness, completeness,
the interrupted dream finally reaching its end this time—
you have little idea how much time has lapsed.
Your youngest daughter peeks in at you
from the doorway and asks if she may have
one of the apples from the kitchen bowl.
Yes, why yes. Would you like it peeled and sliced or whole?

for Theodore Brelsford

First Frost

Emily pouts at her plate of quartered jelly toast,
one side of her face still pink with an impression of sleep
while I move by the clock to get her to preschool and me to work on time.

She crosses her arms, *I don't want it cut*. Knowing she's beyond me in a place
I can't reach, I work to tie up the morning by making our beds and lunches
when suddenly she brightens, *Look at what happened to my plate, Mom!*
which I know without looking holds only the discarded crusts.

But the mood of sleepiness and rushed morning
drags her down again as we put on our heavy jackets.
I zip her zipper and it nicks her neck. *Ouch!*
she cries while I check for blood then hug her tight.

We open the front door—the lawn sparkles with frost,
each blade of grass sticks up like a French-cut green bean.
Emily sweeps down the steps, squats to run
her hands over the frozen green, squeals with delight.

I see this moment through her eyes and want it to last
timeless and large as firsts can in childhood—
the lawn opens up into a field, an unending expanse of play—

but unhappily it's time to go.
I belt her into her car seat,
her small hands red and stinging, get myself settled in the front.

Look, Emily. Our windows are full of tiny ice flowers!
I slide my hands down the steering wheel, rest them in my lap.
We'll take our time, sit silently with the defrost on high,
mesmerized by ice flowers as they disappear detail by intricate detail.

Torn

Reason embraces death,
While out of frightened eyes
Still stares the wish to love.
                    —Theodore Roethke

Nothing right, no place to look or be, the grasses
hum an early fall tune, a slowing heartbeat
following exhilaration.

I sit on my back stoop,
listen to the drain of absence—
water over dry rocks, in garden pots,

under skin and lips sore by forming
what's impossible to state—
Oh, this can't be so!—

when still my senses look out for you,
a walk, how your right foot turns in,
or is it your hip?

a slight unevenness from the back I adore,
a horse's snort as you pass, almost at a run,
by my open or half-shut door—*This is so.*

Discernment

The branches outlined
like pen-and-ink drawing,
the settling sounds of dusk
soften—*end of day*.

Only at the tops of trees
is there movement of air
and beyond, undulating jet trails
accenting the sky while birds
slow down, dismiss all
they have done and left undone.

A siren howls and blips
toward a distant emergency.
Orange and pink tints reflect on cirrus clouds.
The irregular horizon levels in color.
As if tracing a shape, I wait.

Stillness grows interval by interval.
A pale moth flies toward my face then veers.
The streetlights blare. Emily appears
in the light of the back door

her small hands and forehead pressed
against the screen to call me inside—*Mama*.
I answer, *Here I am*. Yes, here I am.

Practice in Gratitude

Sown by a pattern of crisis,
we brace against its aftershock,

its interminable sigh of what's been
dislodged, moves again until it's held.

Now there is no aftershock
and we try to relax the full length of calm.

But soon there is news you are failing
and I make a message of hope: to pull the body whole.

Then you're gone, plucked
out of long suffering, new sorrow.

I step onto the porch,
lift down the hanging fern

where purple martins have nested.
Too soon, too soon. The fledglings flap

and scatter onto the lawn.
I begin the practice of a body in flight they see.

In memoriam, Rita Mayer, 1949–2011

Like This

What do I want?
A stone, a flat stone in a stream
I could stand on to cross.
What would it look like?

An arrangement of shapes I gathered today—
a vine pulled and happily yanked
from a tree, the crazy tendrils grown
out of itself and tangling leaf to leaf,
lazy loop now hung from a railing
of my backyard stoop. Lichen lifted fan by ringed fan
from a rotting log, each demarcation a story like the tree's.
Dried flowers, the shape of feathers,
miniature fletchings, hang like tassels
from their brittle stalks. Mussel shells black
and tinted green by brackish water,
some still hinged, lie open like pairs of miniature lungs.

A turtle nips at the underside
of water to snag a whirligig beetle
and sends a blip of water up
and falls to make the ringed concentric
circles, one after the other. Like this
I would make whole with hands
at the end of my arms, hopeful.

A space in which I'd reveal the raspberry-red moles
on my stomach and chest—
shaped like islands, tiny pursed lips,
the shape a raindrop makes on paper too,
where there's breath in hair, restful.

Things Seen and Unseen

A fog has filled the hollow
behind the house,
layer upon layer of whiteness

that rolls into our eyes
alert for movement of buck or doe
while from beside you I shift

sensing the strength in your neck,
the muscle in your arm,
and watch with you for discernible shapes

as your hand slides down
the length of my hair
to the hollow of my back

and I pull up to you,
rising to kisses,
take your open hand,

come willingly down
the gradual slopes breathless
to walk with you invisible among deer
amazed.

for Jim Stovall

Nobody Dies

Tossed through Virginia
by passenger train,
I sit among Navy recruits
as we pass failing farmhouses.
From one a girl holds
a red ball and balances
between two porch steps.
A man and a woman
stand in the roof's shade.
They wave at us as if we're
old friends always
arriving at the same hour.

At another the steps
are cracked loose.
Two men lean
out of the doorway,
the man in front in a wheelchair,
the other on a crutch.
They wave from the shoulder
as if to reach out and stop us,
invite us inside to talk
of family and friends
they lost and show us
the sagging oceans on their chests,
the same waters of their
limitless dream.

While we approach the station,
I think of past glory,
the linear formation of war.

A bicyclist weaves through
officers stiff in their starched uniforms.
The spokes of his wheels
circle the sun's reflections.

At Cape Henry I am
both witness and victim.
The wreckage of boats
rusts, shell embedded
in rust, hulls where
men may have sat and died.
Fish with their eyes eaten out,
sockets cleaned, fish heads
with their tongues curled
as if in the midst of a curse,
rubbery to the touch, whiten.
Washed-up stingrays, their tails
viscously intact, circle
the blue shell of a crab,
its claw blood red.
A bushel basket stands
upright in an island
of sand and twisted steel,
brown and rust-colored as petrified wood.
A string of fish entrails,
dried like flowers, Japanese lanterns,
clink like thin bone.

In Norfolk the recruits believe
the chaplain who points
and blesses the fleet:
Put your faith in the Lord and He will part the waves for you.
The sound of riggings in the wind, hollow.

Tracing the debris
history has left us,
the bodies not yet clinically
dead dropped into green plastic
bags, tagged and heaped
onto the next helicopter,
the stench of gas, napalm, urine and rats,
of green, foggy and humid green mountains,
of the crawling and oozing death in them,
I know this is the world we cannot
live in or without.
It is wartime. It is peacetime.
It is now.
I will break every bone
in my body to show you
what it is to love.
Watch what shivers under the light.
We fail and forgive,
because nobody dies.

In memoriam, John Clellon Holmes, 1926–1988

All Souls, East Aurora, New York

The maples were never so gold, the fields
never so varied. Staghorn sumac, wild oats,
milkweed pods burst trailing seeds, cattails
among hedgerows of chokecherry, corn drying
tall beside a fallow field, willows yellowing,
the sycamore's spiny fruit set against
the colder blue of the sky, its clouds brightening
high and white. The eastern light slices across
first frost, meets the ground sharply, throws
light and dark to either side like a soul
split it two, a resolving heart's flutter.

In the barn the sweetness of picked
apple and quince, and the cat
stalking the season's change. Bunches
of tied parsley and lavender hang
from the rafters. On a crude windowsill a profusion
of African violet and one purple bloom set aside
in a porcelain creamer, the water soaked up
since placed, perhaps a day ago.
Outside purple finches bob on the feeder.
We follow the taut line of dusk to nightfall,
the chill wash of our flesh,
to keep things whole.

Contraction, Release

Dance is the hidden language of the soul, of the body.
—Martha Graham

The heft of your despair fills me
as I listen to your deepening breath in—
its shallow trailing exhalation. Exiled
from your body I don't know
what to do with my hands.

In a dance my arm becomes
the shape of sorrow, the neck of a blue crane
drinking, the other follows
as the shape of longing, the turning
of its neck tracing a sound—

Centered, both arms lift in unison
from the back becoming the shape
of a crane's wings readied for flight—
they rise lengthening in a column of air
carried to the next by the updraft of their expression.

Revisions

As if home on leave, you show up
at dawn, sneak upstairs
to your room and pull clothes
from your duffel bag to hang them.
You are pulling us out of our homes,
back through the years, and we wake
with you, AWOL, in the family house.

We'd taken you for dead,
killed on a roadway from one
base camp to the next
where you and your buddies
would meet fresh blood.
While monsoons whipped
through the Central Highlands,
a convoy zig-zagged, groaned
and popped gears. We'd taken you as one
of the boys jostled in the back,
suddenly ambushed, shipped home, buried.

The accumulated history since Vietnam
blacks out. We break the rules with you,
accept our return home as natural,
settle into our rooms once more.

But not this time, not for long.
I stand in the doorway of your room, yelling
Where were *you all these years?*
Why didn't you let us know?

The sun sifts from the window.
Your young, tired body stiffens
with a confusion that crosses
your unshaven, handsome face.
There are no answers, only this urge
to shake from you the story of how you

limped through mud and yellow fog
to the base camp that night
and lay on a cot among the staggered
breath of fresh wounded, how your body
fit the depression
left in the mattress by another, how you forgot
what was yours and what was his
by the time you walked out, but it didn't matter,
you were coming home after one, long, lousy mistake.

I enter your room, breathless,
chiming with hangers from both hands.

In memoriam, Stephen Paul Mears, 1950–1969

Jackson Square, New Orleans,
New Year's Eve Following Hurricane Katrina

This year the crowd is so very small,
the weathered locals say, as we choose our places
among dancers, costumed merrymakers,
couples newly in love, stand pinched
in our skins as if in the awkwardness
of a moment before departure, while music bends,
softens then blares like a bad connection near
the end of this weary year, the crowd so very small.

Soon fog begins to wrap the streetlights,
swoops in like ghouls, like genies, like haunts
let loose, as if just outside the muffled light
there's a clear fall into darkness, a void
out of which they rise tonight to cast their spell—
Out of our mouths, dark Katrina, no more.
Back to your first meaning, Katrina, pure.

As if to quicken the countdown to midnight,
fog stands close beside each of us,
touches our skin in whispers, in prayers,
draws us out of our tattered, lonely skins
to embrace the arrival of a new year—
we are so close,
so very close,
furaha again, wishful.

for Roger and Ella McCulloch and family

Under the Weather,
Yaddo, Saratoga Springs, New York

Day 1

The sky flat and expressionless as a blank billboard
blocks the lazy sun. Birds, indecipherable from one
another, cheep and trill among the primordial pines.
A dog sniffs out coded messages from the dirt.
I think of weather moving out, but here clouds
congregate steadily, now a dribble of rain.
The dove's placid triplet sounds.

Day 2

There's no escaping what has lain down overhead, exhausted.
Pine branches hang long and knotted as ancient beards.
James, the groundskeeper, plants another sapling
in the patch of field. The dog circles a woodpile then the sapling,
lifts his leg furtively. A crow lopes out of view.

Day 3

The dog slinks unnaturally low to the ground.
Leaps up. Bites the air in two.

Day 4

The sky lazes, smug in its canopy bed.
The alienable whistle pig rakes the lip of his burrow.
Something is picking daffodils before they bloom.
James rides his tractor into the woods.
A row of rhubarb in the untilled garden sprawls.

Day 5

Thunderstruck. Oh, must we have this weather and weather it too?

Day 6

I raise my ridiculous fists to the sky.
Its muscle flexes.
I spit dirt.
The pines go black.

Days 7 & 8

Okay. So it isn't a personal offense.
One cloud covers the world pole to pole.

Day 9

I admire the whistle pig's patience,
the dog's surreptitiousness,
and James, his daily puttering,
even the pines their primeval establishment.
Oh, but the sky, thou impenetrable one, won't lend
itself to such small pleasures.
Come breaking blue on blue! Show your true, least cantankerous colors!

Day 10

I take a chainsaw to the trees,
clear the stoic horizon.
The dog cracks the whistle pig's underground.
The woodpile burns uproariously.
James and I chew on stalks of rhubarb.
Daffodils bloom in the memory of something—
could it be something like the sun?

Whole Hog

Driving through Little Dime Box, Texas
hog wild, I like to think I hug
the road as you do, wide open speed ahead
with my left leg up on the seat
knee pressed against the car door
the window down and the wind
whipping my hair.
Yes, we want everything in our mouths *now*—

we're the women who got thrown
out of a *poetry* reading for god's sake,
chucked out of The Chukker
for making justified remarks following
each and every bad poem, topped off by my defense
of our good taste with bourbon I threw
into the face of another no-good-writer.
We're the ones who swallowed life whole

dropped our keys and settled in for the ride
no matter how dangerous or wicked or wild.
And lately we've been slowing down—
alert for the red fox that crosses
the back field, we guess the number of pups she feeds,
while in the afternoon sun, high above us at the top of a cottonwood tree
we study a dragonfly perched unmoving
as we float and sip our drinks to the *lap lap lap* of pool water.

Her wings are patterned like an Aztec painting yet translucent
and stiff as if impassioned by a mission—
to settle on the utmost top of the cottonwood and rest
against breeze or enemy, so still we think she's died,
this her last stand, a flag of herself planted in the Texas sky, as we,
moved now and dissipated in our flesh, wait for her signal—
just moments later look again and she's vanished. *Good for her!*
Time for us to head out, girl. See what we can stir up.

for Brenda Bridges

On This Day

His wife had spotted a blimp.
He didn't believe her.
She said, *You'll see.*
He took her shopping bag,
she looked up,
took it upon himself
to walk between her and the curb.
She smiled to the big blue sky.
Just wait. It's huge!
He watched for obstructions,
nudged her around
bottles and trash cans,
noticed blackbirds as they steered
clear of one yellow tricycle.
LOOK! LOOK! she jabbed her finger
straight through the blue.
He was caught instead by the slenderness of her ankles.
She clapped her hands together.
He looked up. *Goodyear* sailed overhead
like a heavenly whale.
He felt himself on its underside,
hands light in the wind,
pointing to a man with a bag
standing beside a woman
against sidewalk traffic.
Their faces open and round.
Cheering.

for Dick Robinson and Lucy Stovall

Once More, Before Dismantling the Dollhouse

Emily has outgrown
the make-believe lives
we created in this two-story house,
neglected since the last episode
played out between us.

I approach taking the house down
room by furnished room, to put into storage,
and I am again Miss Beasley,
the next-door neighbor who always crosses
the side yard bearing a perfect pie
(that's literally attached to her hands)
to her niece's house, enters the side door
into the kitchen and calls, *Oh, Helen*
in her slightly British accent, *Oh, Helen. Yoo-hoo.*
Emily deftly plays everyone else,
except for the boy who's new to the neighborhood;
he's mine.

Miss Beasley's first greeted by one of the many
children (they come and go in number and size)
and the dog that doesn't bark.
Miss Beasley's pie is devoured
right out of her ever-bearing hands.

I'm coming, Helen sighs, disheveled from motherhood.
Miss Beasley pries: *Is Henry here?* (Helen's husband)
When do you expect him? Oh my, what a mess!
she remarks as she moves about the kitchen.

No matter what Helen says or does,
Miss Beasley wants to help out,
so she presses on, begins sweeping.
(We have to ignore the ever-present pie.)
Helen gets a phone call from Henry
at work to meet for lunch. Miss Beasley insists
she'll take the children with dog out to the park.
A flurry of activity ensues; then they all head out the door
with Helen heading up the rear.

Teenager Sarah emerges sullen from her room,
having escaped Miss Beasley's invitation to join them
by feigning sleep, and steps outside into the sun, *free*!
She scales the house in one leap
to the second floor balcony,
and from there to the roof in another.

The new neighbor boy rides up on his Harley.
Hey, how'd you get up there?
It's easy, Sarah replies. *I'll show you.*
She jumps down, takes him by the wrist
and in two leaps lifts them both to the roof
where they sit side-by-side, then a quick, stiff kiss—

when the certainty of touch was still a long way off
but sensed like a vibration, its approach.

Notes

Orr's Island, Maine, August 1959
The Dead Ship of Harpswell mentioned in section II of the poem is a legendary ghost ship in this area of Maine. The appearance of the phantom ship was heralded as an omen of death, and it was believed she was visible only to those directly concerned with the portent.

Furrawn
The title is a Welsh word meaning "talk that leads to intimacy."

Ladder To The Moon
This poem drew its inspiration from Georgia O'Keeffe's *Ladder to the Moon*.

Nobody Dies
John Clellon Holmes introduced me to this ironic expression of war and death. Somebody dies all the time, but few really believe they will be the ones. It is also spoken by Pvt. Rivera in the movie, *A Walk in the Sun*.

Contraction, Release
The title refers to a fundamental modern dance movement in Martha Graham's technique.

Jackson Square, New Orleans,
New Year's Eve Following Hurricane Katrina
Furaha is Swahili, meaning "wishful."

On This Day
Published with "In the Blue, In the Sky" by Martha Wickelhaus as a hand-bound broadside in 1984. The cover woodcut is by Lucy Stovall, who printed the limited edition on an 8 x 12 Chandler & Price press.

Acknowledgments

Many thanks to the editors of the following publications in which some of these poems, in earlier versions, first appeared: *The Akros Review, Brooklyn Review, The GSU Review, Intro 11, The Jabberwock, Slant, Vegetable Box,* and *Xavier Review.*

I gratefully acknowledge my husband, Jim, for his support in making this project a top priority; my sister-in-law, Lucy Stovall, for her numerous talents she brought to this collaboration; David Sanders for his counsel that helped to refine the scope of this selection and for his time and attention to questions of detail; Linda Mizejewski for her belief in my work these many years; both David and Linda for their proofreading and editorial advice; Henry Goodwin for his expertise which brought this volume to completion; Kathleen Mears Carmichael, Jack Carmichael, John Gregory Mears, and Dorothy Mears for their long-lived interest in my writing; and all the others, friends and artists in their own right, who have encouraged me. To borrow a call to action Jim Whitehead used in the closing of his letters—*Onward!*

Madison, Mississippi